Mia Hamm

by Clay Latimer

Reading Consultant:
Dr. Robert Miller
Professor of Special Education
Minnesota State University

CAPSTONE BOOKS
an imprint of Capstone Press
Mankato, Minnesota

Capstone Books are published by Capstone Press
151 Good Counsel Drive, P.O. Box 669, Mankato, Minnesota 56002
http://www.capstone-press.com

Library of Congress Cataloging-in-Publication Data
Latimer, Clay, 1952–
    Mia Hamm/by Clay Latimer.
    p. cm. (Sports heroes)
    Includes bibliographical references (p. 43) and index.
    Summary: A biography of record-breaking soccer player who helped the United
States win a gold medal in soccer in the 1996 Olympics and the Women's World Cup
in 1999.
    ISBN 0-7368-0579-6
    1. Hamm, Mia, 1972—Juvenile literature. 2. Soccer players—United
States—Biography—Juvenile literature. 3. Women soccer players—United
States—Biography—Juvenile literature. [1. Hamm, Mia, 1972–. 2. Soccer players.
3. Women—Biography.] I. Title. II. Sports heroes (Mankato, Minn.)
GV942.7.H27 L27 2001
796.334'092—dc21
[B]   00-023612

Editorial Credits
Matt Doeden, editor; Timothy Halldin, cover designer and illustrator; Heidi Schoof and
    Kimberly Danger, photo researchers

Photo Credits
Active Images, Inc., 16, 26; Jeffrey E. Blackman, 40
Allsport USA, 21, 23, 33; Andy Lyons, 4; Jed Jacobsohn, 6; Stephen Dunn, 19; David
    Cannon, 28; Jamie Squire, 30; Vincent Laforet, 34
AP World Wide Photos, cover
SportsChrome-USA/Bongarts Photography, 9; Rob Tringali Jr., 10, 15, 25, 37, 38,
    45, 46; Bob Tringali, 12

1 2 3 4 5 6 06 05 04 03 02 01

Table of Contents

CHAPTER 1

A Great Summer

It was May 22, 1999. Mia Hamm was playing in a soccer game for the U.S. national team. She knew that it could be one of the most important games of her career. Less than a week earlier, Mia had scored her 107th career goal. One more goal would make her the greatest goal-scorer in international soccer history. This record includes both men and women.

The U.S. team controlled the ball late in the game. Mia took a pass from teammate Cindy Parlow. Mia beat her defender to the right side of the goal and kicked the ball. It sailed past Brazil's goaltender.

Mia's teammates ran onto the field to congratulate her after she scored her 108th goal.

More than 10,000 fans stood to cheer Mia's record. Mia's teammates ran onto the field after the goal to congratulate her. Team captain Carla Overbeck got the ball and handed it to Mia. Mia held the ball over her head and saluted the crowd. The U.S. team went on to win the game.

Mia did not stop there. She played an important role in the championship game of the 1999 Women's World Cup. The U.S. and Chinese teams played this game on July 10. More than 90,000 fans filled the Rose Bowl in Pasadena, California, to watch. Millions of people around the world watched on television. The game was one of the biggest events in the history of women's team sports.

Mia and her teammates played good defense throughout the game. But they could not score a goal. Neither team scored during regulation time. The teams played two scoreless overtimes. The game then came down to a five-goal shootout.

Mia took the fourth kick for the United States. She scored a goal. Mia's goal gave teammate Brandi Chastain a chance to win the

Mia led the U.S. national team to a win over China in the 1999 Women's World Cup.

game on the final kick. Chastain scored a goal and the game was over. The United States had won the shootout 5-4. Mia and her teammates were the Women's World Cup champions.

About Mia Hamm

Mia Hamm is one of the biggest stars in women's athletics today. She is one of the most important members of the U.S. national team. Her teammates rely on her skills and leadership on and off the field.

Mia has been a soccer player most of her life. She joined the national team at age 15. Mia also played college soccer at the University of North Carolina (UNC). She even led the U.S. team to an Olympic gold medal in 1996.

Mia has millions of fans around the world. Girls and boys around the world own posters and T-shirts with Mia's picture on them. Mia also has appeared in TV commercials. She appeared in a Nike commercial with basketball star Michael Jordan. Some people have even compared Mia's popularity with Jordan's.

CAREER STATISTICS

Mia Hamm

International Statistics

Year	Games	Starts	Goals	Assists	Points
1987	7	4	0	0	0
1988	8	7	0	0	0
1989	1	0	0	0	0
1990	5	1	4	1	9
1991	28	24	10	4	24
1992	2	2	1	0	2
1993	16	16	10	4	24
1994	9	9	10	5	25
1995	21	20	19	18	56
1996	23	23	9	18	36
1997	16	16	18	6	42
1998	21	21	20	20	60
1999	26	26	13	16	42
Totals	183	169	114	92	320

CHAPTER 2

The Early Years

Mia Hamm was born March 17, 1972, in Selma, Alabama. Her parents are Stephanie and Bill Hamm. Mia is the fourth of six children. Mia's given name is Mariel. But Stephanie called her Mia after Stephanie's former ballet teacher.

Bill was a U.S. Air Force pilot. The family moved to many different air force bases during Mia's childhood. They lived in places such as California, Texas, Virginia, and Italy. Bill became a soccer fan when he lived in Italy. The sport is very popular there. Bill took a job as a part-time soccer coach in Italy. He

---

Mia has enjoyed soccer nearly her whole life.

Mia has played in soccer leagues since she was 5 years old.

also taught his children to play and enjoy the sport.

Young Mia

Mia learned about soccer at an early age. When she was 1 year old, Mia saw children playing soccer on a street near her home. Mia began walking toward the children. She wanted to play. But Stephanie stopped her. Stephanie did not want Mia to get hurt.

Four years later, Stephanie wanted Mia to take ballet lessons. But Mia did not want to learn ballet. She wanted to play soccer instead.

Mia played in many youth soccer leagues over the next few years. She played for both girls' and boys' teams. She was a great goal-scorer even when she was young. Her speed and skill showed on the field. Mia even tried officiating some youth soccer games. But she did not like officiating. She thought the players' parents yelled too much.

Garrett Hamm

Mia's hero was her older brother, Garrett. The Hamm family adopted Garrett when Mia was 5 years old. Garrett was a Thai-American. He was three years older than Mia.

Mia and Garrett got along very well. Mia followed her brother around. The two enjoyed spending time together. Both Mia and Garrett enjoyed playing and watching soccer. Garrett was a good soccer player. Mia and Garrett enjoyed watching one another's games.

In 1997, Garrett died from a rare blood disease called aplastic anemia. He was 28 years old. Mia now has her own model of shoes made by the Nike company. Garrett's initials are on the bottom of every pair.

High School

People began to recognize Mia's soccer talent when she was in high school. At age 14, she played for Notre Dame High School in Wichita Falls, Texas. The Hamm family later moved to Virginia. There, Mia played for Lake Braddock Secondary School in Burke, Virginia. She was named an All American. This award meant she was one of the best girls' soccer players in the United States.

College coaches began to notice Mia when she was 14. That year, a coach named Anson Dorrance from the University of North Carolina heard about Mia. He went to Texas to see Mia play. When Dorrance saw Mia, he knew that she could be a star.

Mia gained many of her soccer skills while playing in youth leagues.

CHAPTER 3

Mia's Big Break

Dorrance was surprised by Mia's speed and skills. He said that he had never seen so much speed in a women's soccer game.

The U.S. National Team

In 1987, Dorrance helped Mia gain a spot on the U.S. national team. Mia was only 15 when she joined the team. She was the youngest woman ever to play on the team.

Mia played in three Olympic Festivals during the late 1980s and early 1990s. These events helped U.S. Olympic officials decide who would play in the Olympics. Mia's teams

Anson Dorrance said Mia was the fastest women's player he had ever seen.

won gold medals in two of these Olympic Festivals. Her team won a silver medal in the other festival.

Mia was the youngest member of the U.S. national team when it won the Women's World Cup in 1991. She was 19 years old. Mia was a starter in five of the six games in the championship competition. She played fullback because another player was injured. She was not used to the position. But Mia still scored two goals in the tournament.

Early College Years

In 1989, Mia joined Dorrance at the University of North Carolina. UNC's team name is the Tarheels. Mia was an immediate success there. In her first year, Mia scored 21 goals. She helped the Tarheels win the national championship.

In 1990, Mia played an important part in a playoff match for another national championship. UNC was playing North

Mia's play on the national team eventually gave her a chance to play in the Olympics.

Carolina State University (N.C. State) in a quarterfinal match. The Tarheels had trailed in the regulation period before coming back to tie the game. N.C. State took another lead in the overtime period. But UNC tied the game again.

Mia then kicked a curving corner kick with only two minutes remaining in overtime. Teammate Rita Tower deflected Mia's kick into N.C. State's goal to give the Tarheels the win. Some people still call this the most exciting game in the history of women's soccer.

Mia and her teammates went on to win their last two games of the 1990 season. These victories gave the team another national championship.

A College Star

Mia did not play for UNC in 1991. She spent that year playing for the U.S. national team. But she returned to college soccer in 1992. That year, she became one of the greatest college soccer players ever.

Mia quickly became a star for the University of North Carolina.

Mia led the Tarheels to one of the best years a college soccer team has ever had. The team had a 25-0 record. They outscored their opponents by a total of 132-11. Mia scored 32 goals and had 33 assists. With a total of 97 points, she had scored more points than any other U.S. women's soccer player. Her 33 assists set a new NCAA record.

Mia scored three goals to lead the Tarheels to a 9-1 win over Duke University in the 1992 NCAA championship game. It was her third national championship with the Tarheels. Mia was named National Player of the Year.

In 1993, Mia won another National Player of the Year award. She also led UNC to another national championship. Mia scored 68 points that year. She had 26 goals and 16 assists.

Mia graduated from college in 1993. She finished her college career with 278 points. No other player in NCAA history has scored that many points. Mia scored 103 goals and 72 assists during college. These achievements

Mia was named National Player of the Year in 1992.

are NCAA records. In 1994, UNC retired Mia's number. No other UNC women's soccer player ever will wear her number 19 jersey.

Personal Life

Mia did not just play soccer during college. She spent much of her time studying. Mia earned a degree in political science. She learned about governments and history. But finding time for practicing, studying, and games was not easy. She studied before and after games. She even studied on flights to and from games.

Mia also met her husband at UNC. His name is Christiaan Corry. Christiaan also was a UNC student. Mia and Christiaan married in 1994. Christiaan now serves as a pilot in the U.S. Marine Corps.

Mia returned to the U.S. national team after college.

CHAPTER 4

The World Game

After college, Mia again played for the U.S. national team. By 1994, many people considered her to be the best women's soccer player in the United States. That year, she was named U.S. Soccer's Female Athlete of the Year. Some people believed Mia was the best women's player in the world.

The 1995 Season
The United States had high hopes entering the 1995 Women's World Cup in Sweden. Many people believed the United States had the best team in the tournament. But the team lost to Norway 1-0 in the semifinals.

By 1994, many people thought Mia was the best women's soccer player in the United States.

Despite the loss, Mia had a good season. She led the team with 19 goals and 18 assists. She also helped the team win the U.S. Cup tournament. Mia scored a goal on a free kick in the championship game against Norway. The United States won the game 2-1. Mia was named MVP of the tournament. She also won a second U.S. Soccer's Female Athlete of the Year award.

The 1996 Olympics

Women's soccer became a regular Olympic event in 1996. Mia was selected to play on the first U.S. Olympic team. She scored a goal in the United States' first game against Denmark. But Mia twisted her ankle in a game against Sweden. She had to leave the field. The injury caused Mia to miss the team's next game against China.

Mia returned to action for the championship tournament. She helped the United States beat Norway 2-1. The win sent the team to the gold-medal game against China.

Mia and her teammates won the gold medal at the 1996 Olympics.

Mia played hard against China. She set up a goal that gave the United States an early 1-0 lead. China later tied the game 1-1. Mia helped to set up another U.S. goal. The team was ahead 2-1. But Mia hurt her ankle again late in the game. She was helped off the field.

The U.S. team held its lead after Mia left the field. Mia and her teammates won the first gold medal in Olympic women's soccer. Later that year, Mia won her third straight U.S. Soccer's Female Athlete of the Year award.

The 1999 World Cup

The 1999 season did not start well for Mia. She did not score any goals in her first eight games. But she soon broke out of her scoring slump and had one of her greatest seasons ever.

The United States hosted the 1999 Women's World Cup. Mia and her teammates wanted to win the championship in front of U.S. soccer fans. The team had to win six games to win the championship.

Almost 79,000 fans attended the United States' first game of the 1999 Women's World Cup.

The United States' first game was against Denmark. It took place in New Jersey. Almost 79,000 fans attended the game. The players needed a police escort to move safely through the crowds. Mia scored the first goal of the game. She helped her team to a 3-0 victory.

The United States' next game was in Chicago against Nigeria. More than 65,000 fans filled the stadium. But the fans were surprised when Nigeria scored a goal only two minutes into the game. Mia and her teammates remained calm. Mia set up a U.S. goal to tie the game. She then scored a goal. The U.S. team went on to win the game 7-1.

The U.S. team kept winning. The team beat North Korea 3-0. The next game was against Germany. Germany had a 2-1 lead at halftime. But the United States came back in the second half to win 3-2. Next, the United States defeated Brazil 2-0 to advance to the championship game against China. The teams

Mia met President Bill Clinton and his family after the U.S. team won the 1999 Women's World Cup.

played to a 0-0 tie in regulation. But the U.S. team won the game 5-4 on penalty kicks.

Mia and her teammates went on a victory tour after winning the Women's World Cup. They appeared on TV shows. The team members even met President Bill Clinton at the White House.

CHAPTER 5

Mia Hamm Today

Mia continues to be an important part of the U.S. national team. She is a hero to millions of young girls and boys. She also is one of the most recognized female athletes in the world.

Off the Field

Mia stays busy when she is not playing soccer. She is involved in a charity called the Marrow Foundation. She helps the organization teach others about bone marrow transplants. These operations help people

Mia is one of the most recognized female athletes in the world.

with blood diseases such as the one her brother Garrett died from. The Marrow Foundation also helps to register people as bone marrow donors.

In 1999, Mia formed the Mia Hamm Foundation. This organization raises money for bone marrow research. The money helps doctors and scientists learn how bone marrow transplants can save lives.

In 1998, Mia organized the first Garrett Game in honor of her brother. Members of the U.S. national team play against a group of top female college players in this game. Money earned from the Garrett Game goes to bone marrow research.

More Soccer

Mia plans to continue playing soccer in the future. She remains one of the best players on the U.S. national team. She looks forward to winning future championships and Olympic gold medals.

Mia looks forward to winning future championships with the U.S. national team.

In late 1999, Mia and her teammates threatened to stop playing for the U.S. national team. The women demanded pay equity with the players on the U.S. men's team. The players on the men's team earned more money than the players on the women's team. Mia and her teammates felt that all U.S. soccer players should receive the same pay.

At first, the U.S. Soccer Federation did not want to increase the pay for the women. But Mia and her teammates were firm.

In February 2000, the U.S. Soccer Federation agreed to the players' demands. Soccer players on the U.S. women's and men's teams now receive equal pay. Many people believe that this is an important achievement in the history of women's sports.

Today, players on the U.S. men's and women's teams receive equal pay.

Career Highlights

1972—Mia is born on March 17 in Selma, Alabama.

1987—Mia makes her first appearance in an international game.

1989—Mia plays her first year for UNC. The team wins the NCAA championship.

1990—Mia scores her first international goal against Norway. UNC wins another NCAA championship.

1991—Mia plays on the U.S. team that wins the first Women's World Cup.

1992—Mia sets NCAA records in points, goals, and assists. She wins the National Player of the Year award and leads North Carolina to a 25-0 record and an NCAA championship.

1993—Mia wins her second National Player of the Year award and helps her team to another NCAA championship.

1994—Mia wins her first U.S. Soccer's Female Athlete of the Year award.

1995—The U.S. team finishes third in the World Cup.

1996—Mia helps the U.S. team win the Olympic gold medal.

1999—Mia becomes soccer's all-time leading scorer. The United States wins the Women's World Cup.

Words to Know

bone marrow (BOHN MA-roh)—a soft substance inside bones; bone marrow helps the body produce blood cells.

equity (EH-kwi-tee)—equal treatment for two or more groups

political science (puh-LIT-uh-kuhl SYE-uhnss)—the study of governments and the political process

quarterfinal (kwor-tur-FYE-nuhl)—a game played in a tournament when eight teams remain in competition; winners of quarterfinal games advance to a semifinal game.

semifinal (SEM-ee-fye-nuhl)—a game played in a tournament when four teams remain in competition; winners of semifinal games advance to the finals.

slump (SLUHMP)—a period of time in which an athlete does not perform as well as normal

To Learn More

Brill, Marlene Targ. *Winning Women in Soccer*. Sport Success. Hauppauge, N.Y.: Barron's, 1999.

Dougherty, Terri. *Mia Hamm*. Jam Session. Minneapolis: Abdo, 2000.

Kirkpatrick, Rob. *Mia Hamm, Soccer Star*. New York: PowerKids Press, 2000.

Rutledge, Rachel. *Mia Hamm: Striking Superstar*. Soccer's New Wave. Brookfield, Conn.: Millbrook Press, 2000.

Useful Addresses

The Marrow Foundation
400 Seventh Street NW
Suite 206
Washington, DC 20004

Mia Hamm Foundation
P.O. Box 56
Chapel Hill, NC 27514

U.S. Soccer Federation
1811 South Prairie Avenue
Chicago, IL 60616

Internet Sites

Mia Hamm Foundation
http://www.miafoundation.org

Soccer America
http://www.socceramerica.com

U.S. Soccer
http://www.us-soccer.com

Women's Soccer World—Mia Hamm
http://www.womensoccer.com/biogs/hamm.html

Index